UNDERSTANDI

MW01490019

Ten Minutes With GOD

UNDERSTANDING GOD

Can I Trust Him?

10 MINUTES WITH GOD: UNDERSTANDING GOD
Can I Trust Him?

ISBN - Paperback: 9798311660297
First Edition: February 2025
Printed in the United States of America.

For more information or to book an event, contact :
Janine McNally, B. Ed., Th. M., D. Min.
Panama City, FL 32401

Equipping Fireflies, Inc.
Janine@EquippingFireflies.com

CONTENTS

A MESSAGE TO PARENTS

Dear Parent:

It's not enough to raise your children physically. Your greatest task is to raise them spiritually - to know and follow God.

Most parents are aware of their responsibility but don't know how to fulfill it. "Ten-Minutes with God" is a series of books that are an easy-to-use, practical resource designed to help parents disciple their children and build the habit of spending time with God. It is the perfect way to embark on the Biblical journey of passing down faith to your children and grandchildren.

Just ten minutes each day.

THE BIBLICAL MANDATE

Research tells us that most parents do not invest in the discipleship of their children. Faith is more of an afterthought rather than a priority. Have you asked yourself, "What is my plan?" "Where do I want my children to be in twenty years?" "What is my goal for them – a sports scholarship, a prestigious school, a high-paying career?"

Do you know it is YOUR job to teach, encourage and lead your children to know and follow God?
Do you have a plan?

The overwhelming feedback regarding parents' responsibility to disciple their children is that while they want to, they lack the confidence to do a good job and feel inadequate. The common response is to let the "experts" do it! They have been trained, biblically educated, and know what they're doing!

It's easy to abdicate your responsibility to the church. To delegate it to the "experts." However, the Bible teaches quite the opposite. It is not their job. It's yours!

THE BIBLE ASSUMES FAMILY.

The Shema (Deuteronomy 6) is a prayer central to Judaism. Recited twice daily, it is as familiar to the Jewish people of Israel as John 3:16 is to Christians.

"These commandments that I give you today are to be on your hearts. **Impress them on your children**.
Talk about them when you sit at home, when you walk along the road, when you lie down, and when you get up.

You shall **bind them as a sign on your hand**, and they shall be as **frontlets between your eyes**. You shall **write them on the doorposts** of your house and on your gates."

Deuteronomy 6:8-9 [NIV].[1]

The Bible is clear.
We are to "**impress**" God's word on our children.
Other translations say, "You shall teach them **diligently**."

"Diligently" is the translation of a Hebrew word that has the meaning of "repeat" or "say again and again." We are to teach God's Word to our children and repeat it, repeat it, repeat it.

When do we do that?
By making it a part of our daily lives.
God's truth can be impressed in intentional, scheduled ways or in those informal, unplanned moments when we "sit," "walk," or "lie down."

We can talk about them…

- When you sit at home (e.g., family devotions).
- When you walk along the road (e.g., walks to the park).
- When you lie down (e.g., nighttime prayers).
- When you get up (e.g., praying before the day begins).

For example,

- When we walk in the park and see a beautiful tree, we can "impress" our children with God's amazing creation.
- Or, on the car ride to sports practice, we can play a song from a playlist we created to help us learn memory verses.
- We can put our phones down at the dinner table and use conversation starters to generate discussion about what happened at school and encourage our children to trust when hard times come.

We can…

- Bind them as a sign on your hand, and they shall be as frontlets between your eyes – like wearing a WWJD[2] bracelet or a cross necklace.
- Write them on the doorposts of your house - the first thing we see when we leave and when we come home.
- Write them on your "gates" so our neighbors can see.

This transfer of faith "is to be interwoven throughout daily conversation."[3] The family becomes the classroom. When children ask questions, parents can turn them into teachable moments. We are not only responsible for teaching our children but are also commanded to do so with our grandchildren.

Notice the message that Moses gives parents and grandparents.

"That the generation to come [children] might know them,
the children who would be born [grandchildren], that they may arise
and declare them to their children [great grandchildren]."
Psalm 78:6.[4]

So, Grandma and Grandpa – just because you have finished raising your children, your responsibility continues with your grandbabies!

What are we to teach?

"…and he [Moses] said to them: "Set your hearts on **all the words**
which I testify among you today, which you shall command
your children to be careful to observe - all the words of this law."
Deuteronomy 32:46.

We are to teach God's commandments so our children will learn to obey and follow God.

Homes are the perfect place to take advantage of those teachable moments, and parents are the ideal people.

It's NOT the church's job.

The biblical mandate falls on the parents (literally, the father) to raise their children in the nurture and admonition of the Lord.

"And you, **fathers**, do not provoke your children to wrath,
but **bring them up in the training and admonition of the Lord."**
Ephesians 6:4.

The Bible never tells parents to take their children to the temple [church], nor does it instruct the church to teach children.
It is NOT the church's job.

> "The failure of parents to disciple their children is nothing new," but what is new is "the overwhelming, false, and unbiblical belief that regular participation in modern church life is equated with fulfilling their responsibility toward their child's discipleship."[5]

And the sobering thought is that **parents** will be held accountable by God (**not the church**).

Parents: Take your responsibility seriously.

WHAT ELSE CAN PARENTS DO?

Model Your Faith at Home.

One of the most important things parents can do is model their faith in their daily lives. When worship songs are replaced with cursing and gossip and the Bible is never opened, faith erodes alongside growing disillusionment. If children observe their parents playing "church," attending because it's socially acceptable but displaying no evidence of their faith during the week, all their children will see is a display of hypocrisy.

Prioritize Church Attendance

When families begin to habitually skip church, for whatever reason, they are heading towards a slippery slope. They are sending a message to their children that church [and God] is not a priority. Other activities are given precedence, and the church is just another option for how to spend a Sunday morning.

Parents whose own commitment is minimal are likely to raise children with a similarly shallow, unnurtured faith. If their child's faith exists, their convictions will likely crumble under the world's inevitable challenges and pressures that will surely come their way.

HOW TO USE THIS BOOK

This book was written to help parents disciple their children and build the habit of spending time with God. It's the perfect way to embark on the Biblical journey of passing down your faith to your children and your children's children.

Each "Ten-Minutes with God" book includes 20 short devotions, enough for a month (five cards each week). Read a devotion with your child each night (or morning).

Day 1-5: Monday through Friday. Read one devotion each day.

Day 6: Saturday is a catch–up day. For kids who didn't miss a weekday, a fun activity is provided to reinforce the lessons from that week.

Day 7: Sunday – Talk about what you learned in church.

Each devotion includes:

- A different fun Conversation Starter.
- A Bible verse or passage to read.
- A short devotion.
- A space for a Journal entry.
- A Prayer Prompt.

This devotion book is designed for individual use (by a child old enough to read well) or as a family devotion tool. They were written for children ages 7-12 but can be used with younger children – they might need mom or dad to help.

Each book also includes:

- Two memory verses with scannable QR codes linked to a catchy Bible memory song.
- An Answer Key for any fill-in-the-blank questions.

SYMBOLS

FUN QUESTION: Read the fun Conversation Starter and allow time for your child to answer.

READ: Read the Bible verses for the day. Look them up in an age-appropriate Bible.[6]

READ the devotional thought and answer any questions (see answer cards).

WRITE: Help your child write down what they learned in the journal space provided.

LEARN: Take time each day to review the Memory Verse together. Scan the QR code for a fun, upbeat song.

PRAY: Pray together. Record your child's prayer requests and answers and review them often.

Make it a goal to complete all seven books.

1. Understanding God – Can I Trust Him?
2. Knowing God - Can I Know for Sure?
3. Following God – What Do I Do?
4. Understanding the Bible – How Do I Know it's True?
5. Understanding Me (Identity) – Who Am I?
6. Understanding Big Questions – I Need Answers.
7. Understanding Life & Death – What Happens When We Die?

MEMORY VERSES

"Believe in the Lord Jesus Christ, and you will be saved."

Acts 16:31.

SCAN ME

"Trust in the Lord with all your heart and lean not
on your own understanding;
in all your ways submit to Him,
and He will make your paths straight."

Proverbs 3:5-6.

SCAN ME

WEEK ONE

Who is God?

God is Omnipresent.

God is Omniscient.

MONDAY

FUN QUESTION: Who would you pick if you could switch places with anyone for a day? Why did you choose that person?

READ: Hebrews 11:1-3.

READ the devotion below.

WHO IS GOD?

I know I could never trade places with God, but I would sure love to know what He's like. I'm betting that you have lots of questions, too. The good news is that the Bible tells us all about Him.

It is very normal to have questions about God. People tell us to "trust God, " but it's not easy to trust someone you cannot see. You might wonder:

- How do you know He's there?
- Can He really hear us when we pray?
- What is He really like?

Trusting what you cannot see is called "**faith**." The Bible says that faith is being **sure** of what we do not see.[7]

A good example of faith is the wind. Although you can't see the wind, you can see the trees moving and the ocean waves breaking. The same is true of God. Although you can't see Him, you can see Him working in people's lives.

So, how do you trust something you cannot see? How can we be sure of God?
It takes faith.

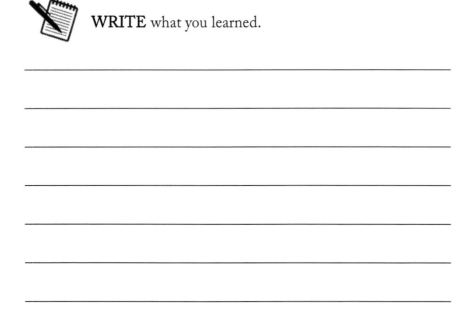

WRITE what you learned.

LEARN: Begin to learn Acts 16:31.

SCAN ME

PRAY: Ask God to help you learn more about Him.

Write your prayer requests and any answers below.

PRAYER REQUESTS:

ANSWERS to PRAYERS:

TUESDAY

FUN QUESTION: If you could have one superpower, what would it be?

READ: Psalm 19:1.

READ the devotion below.

WHAT IS GOD LIKE?

God has many "superpowers!" But we don't know everything about Him.

For example, we don't know what God looks like because He is invisible. He doesn't have a body like we do. But we can look around the world and see what He is like through His **creation**.

We can see God's **gentleness** in the delicate petals of a flower.

Or a nest of soft baby bunnies.

We can see His **strength** in the force of the ocean waves.

Or the tall, snowy mountain ranges.

We can see His **creativity** in the variety of plants and animals He made.

So, we might not be able to see God, but we know He is there because we can see what He does.

WRITE what you learned.

LEARN: Keep learning Acts 16:31.

PRAY: Pray for your family. Write your prayer requests, look back at your past requests, and write any answers below.

PRAYER REQUESTS:

ANSWERS to PRAYERS:

WEDNESDAY

FUN QUESTION: Who is someone you'd really like to meet?

READ: Psalm113:4-6.

READ the devotion below.

GOD IS OMNIPRESENT

Would you like to meet God? That would be pretty cool. The amazing thing is that we can.

While we are waiting to meet Him, we can read all about Him. The Bible tells us all about God. It teaches us that God is **everywhere**, so we can talk to him whenever we want. He is **Omnipresent**.

The word "Omnipresent" is made up of two Latin words:

"Omni" (meaning "all" or "every") + "Present."

So, "omnipresent" means that God is "all-present."

- God is in all places at all times.
- He lives in Heaven and is also here with us on Earth.

And He is always watching out for us!

How does it make you feel to know that God is always watching?

God sees us when we are at our best AND when we are not.

The good news is that He loves us, no matter what.

WRITE what you learned.

LEARN: Keep learning Acts 16:31.

PRAY: Pray for your friends. Write your prayer requests, look back at your past requests, and write any answers below.

PRAYER REQUESTS:

ANSWERS to PRAYERS:

THURSDAY

FUN QUESTION: If you could have a magical ability, like flying or invisibility, what would it be?

READ: Psalm 139:7-10.

READ the devotion below.

GOD IS OMNIPRESENT (Part Two)

Did you know that we are never alone? One of God's "magical" powers is that He is always present. Do you remember the big word from yesterday? God is "Omnipresent." He is with us wherever we go and promises to be with us no matter what.

Where is God? Check the correct answers.

- ☐ In the heavens?
- ☐ In the depths of the earth?
- ☐ In the sunrise?
- ☐ On the edge of the sea?
- ☐ In the darkness?
- ☐ In the light?
- ☐ In your classroom?
- ☐ In your bedroom?

READ the last part of Hebrews 13:5.

What does God promise? God will **NEVER** L _ _ _ _ you.

WRITE what you learned.

LEARN: Keep learning Acts 16:31.

SCAN ME

PRAY: Pray for your Grandparents. Write your prayer requests, look back at your past requests, and write any answers below.

PRAYER REQUESTS:

ANSWERS to PRAYERS:

FRIDAY

FUN QUESTION: What would you buy if you won a million dollars?

READ: Isaiah 46:9-11.

READ the devotion below.

GOD IS OMNISCIENT

A million dollars would be nice, but I think it would be even better if you could know EVERYTHING... everything that was happening now and everything that would happen in the future. You would have enough knowledge to easily replace that million dollars.

The Bible tells us that God knows everything.
He is omniscient. "Omniscient" is another big word made up of two Latin words.

"OMNI" + "SCIENT"

Do you remember what "Omni" means? ___ ___ ___.

"Scientia" looks a bit like the word "Science." It is Latin for "knowledge."

So, God has "ALL KNOWLEDGE."

God knows before things happen. He decides how things will end. His plans will always succeed, and He will do whatever He wants.

God knows the B __ __ __ __ __ __ __ __ from the E __ __.
And He knows everything in between!

I want God on my side! Don't you?

WRITE what you learned.

LEARN: Fill in the words to your memory verse.

"B __ __ __ __ __ __ in the Lord Jesus Christ,

and you will be S __ __ __ __."

A __ __ __ 16:31.

PRAY: Pray for your school teachers. Write your prayer requests, look back at your past requests, and write any answers below.

PRAYER REQUESTS:

ANSWERS to PRAYERS:

SATURDAY.

Today is a catch-up day.

If you are all caught up, here is a fun activity for you to do.

Who is God?

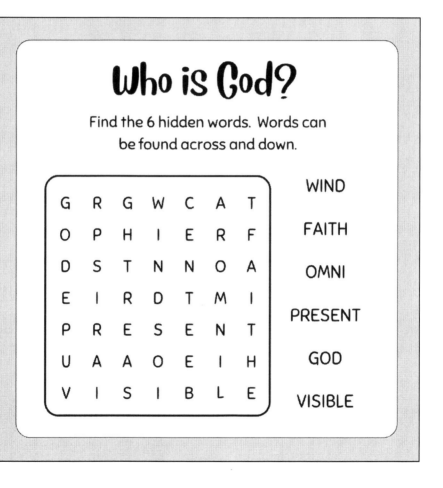

Find the 6 hidden words. Words can be found across and down.

G	R	G	W	C	A	T
O	P	H	I	E	R	F
D	S	T	N	N	O	A
E	I	R	D	T	M	I
P	R	E	S	E	N	T
U	A	A	O	E	I	H
V	I	S	I	B	L	E

WIND

FAITH

OMNI

PRESENT

GOD

VISIBLE

SUNDAY.

Talk about what you learned in church and/or Sunday School and write it down below.

WEEK TWO

God is Omniscient (Part Two),

God is Omnipotent.

The Trinity.

MONDAY

FUN QUESTION: If you could be a celebrity, what would you want to be famous for?

READ: Psalm 147:3-5.

READ the devotion below.

GOD IS OMNISCIENT (Part Two)

There are many celebrities in the world, such as famous singers, movie stars, or even world leaders. But none of them are omniscient! Do you remember what that means?

"Omni" = All "Scient" = Knowledge.

When we say that God is Omniscient, it means that

God knows E _ _ _ _ _ _ _ _ _.

Isn't it comforting to know that God knows EVERYthing?
He knows yesterday, today, and tomorrow.

He knows what has already happened in the past and what will happen in the future.

And we can trust Him with everything!
He is better than any celebrity.

WRITE what you learned.

____

____

____

____

____

____

LEARN: Fill in the words to your memory verse.

"B _ _ _ _ _ _ in the Lord Jesus C _ _ _ _ _,

and you will be S _ _ _ _."

A _ _ _ 16:31.

PRAY: Pray for your church. Write your prayer requests, look back at your past requests, and write any answers below.

PRAYER REQUESTS:

ANSWERS to PRAYERS:

TUESDAY

FUN QUESTION: If you had your own personal genie, what would you wish for?

READ: Jeremiah 32:17.

READ the devotion below.

GOD IS OMNIPOTENT

If you could have any wish, would you wish to be powerful? The Bible tells us that God is Omnipotent.

I bet you can figure out what this word means without any help.

"Omni" = "All"

"Potent" = "To have great power."

The Bible teaches us that God is ALL-POWERFUL.
He can do anything that He wants to do.
Nothing or nobody is stronger than God.

One of the most amazing ways God showed His power was by creating the world. He created everything **from nothing**. Now, that's POWER!

WRITE what you learned.

SCAN ME

LEARN: Fill in the words to your memory verse.

"B _ _ _ _ _ _ in the L _ _ _ Jesus C _ _ _ _ _,

and you W _ _ _ be S _ _ _ _."

A _ _ _ 16:31.

PRAY: Pray for your Sunday School teacher. Write your prayer requests, look back at your past requests, and write any answers below.

PRAYER REQUESTS:

ANSWERS to PRAYERS:

WEDNESDAY

FUN QUESTION: If you were the president, what new laws would you make? Which ones would you ditch?

READ: Isaiah 40:21-23.

READ the devotion below.

GOD IS OMNIPOTENT (Part Two)

God is stronger than any president or ruler. He can defeat any enemy that we might face. God is strong and mighty!

READ Isaiah 40:23 again.

He brings P __ __ __ __ __ __ __ and R __ __ __ __ __ __ to nothing.

READ Job 12:10.

God holds our lives in His H __ __ __ __.

READ Psalm 24:8.

God is S__ __ __ __ __ and M__ __ __ __ __ in B__ __ __ __ __.

God understands everything about us and can handle anything! He is ALL present, ALL knowing, and ALL powerful!
Isn't that amazing?

Our lives are safely in His hands.

WRITE what you learned.

____

____

____

____

____

____

LEARN: Keep learning Acts 16:31.

"B _ _ _ _ _ _ in the L _ _ _ Jesus C _ _ _ _ _,

and you W _ _ _ be S _ _ _ _."

A _ _ _ 16:31.

PRAY: Pray for your enemies.

Sometimes, the last thing we want is to pray for those who are mean or hurtful. But the Bible tells us that the best thing we can do is to pray for them.

Find Matthew 5:44 in your Bible and fill in the blanks.

"But I tell you, ___ ___ ___ ___ your enemies and ___ ___ ___ ___ for those who persecute you."

Write your prayer requests, look back at your past requests, and write any answers below.

PRAYER REQUESTS:

ANSWERS to PRAYERS:

THURSDAY

FUN QUESTION: Name someone you trust. Why do you trust them?

READ: Deuteronomy 6:4-6.

READ the devotion below.

THERE IS ONLY ONE GOD.

You might trust your mom or dad. You might trust your best friend. The Bible teaches that God can be trusted.

The Bible also says that there is only ONE God.
Some religions believe in other gods, but the Bible teaches there is only ONE true God.
There is one God, and there is no one like Him.

READ Isaiah 46:9.

"There is N _ _ _ _ _ like Me."

There are many things that we don't understand about God.
He is God, and we are not.

The good news is that God can be trusted - more than anyone else - because He is perfect - no mistakes!
We can trust people, but eventually, they will make mistakes and let us down.

But God won't!

WRITE what you learned.

LEARN: Write Acts 16:31 from memory (if you can!).

SCAN ME

"B _ _ _ _ _ _ in the L _ _ _ J _ _ _ _

C _ _ _ _ _, and you W _ _ _ be S _ _ _ _."

A _ _ _ 16:31.

PRAY: Ask God to help you learn more about Him. Write your prayer requests, look back at your past requests, and write any answers below.

PRAYER REQUESTS:

ANSWERS to PRAYERS:

FRIDAY

FUN QUESTION: If you had unlimited resources ($$$), what would you buy?

READ: Matthew 28:19.

READ the devotion below.

GOD IS THREE PERSONS IN ONE.

No matter what we would buy, "things" never last forever. We could be gazillionaires, but it wouldn't last. Nothing we buy lasts.

When we have God on our side, we have more resources available than we will ever need. God is unlimited in what He has and in who He is. God is limitless.

Remember that yesterday, we talked about the Bible teaching that there is only ONE God.

Well, the Bible also teaches that God is actually THREE Persons in ONE. The technical term for this is the "Trinity."

Do you know what "TRI" means?

What do these things have in common?

Tri-cycle? ___ ___ ___ ___ ___ wheels.

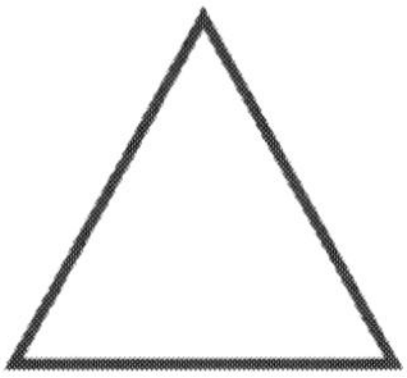

Tri-angle? ___ ___ ___ ___ ___ sides.

Tri-pod? ___ ___ ___ ___ ___ legs.

God is three Persons in one.

This is one of the most difficult things to understand about God. Our brains cannot fully understand everything about God. If they could, we would be God.

There is:

1. God the F _ _ _ _ _.
2. God the S _ _.
3. God the H _ _ _ S _ _ _ _ _.

Each Person is GOD but is unique, with a specific job.

Some people have tried to explain the Trinity in these ways.

1. The Trinity is Like an Egg.

Three different parts: the shell, the white, and the yoke.

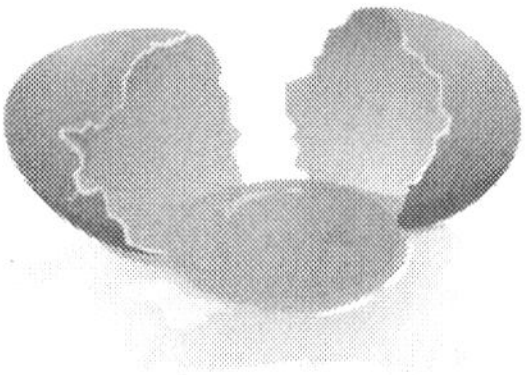

2. The Trinity is like an apple.

Three different parts – the skin, the flesh, and the seed.

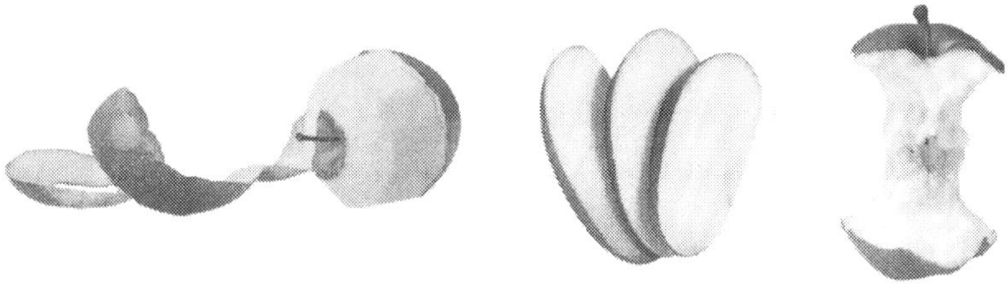

3. The Trinity is like a Three-Leaf Clover

But God is not divided into three parts. Each person of the Trinity is fully God, all on their own.

4. The Trinity is Like Water.

It can be a liquid (to drink), a solid (like ice), or a gas (steam).

5. The Trinity is like the Celtic Trinity Knot

The Celtic Trinity Knot has three distinct loops in the design. But when you trace the loop pattern, there is no beginning or end. It's all one connected line!

These are helpful ways to try to understand this mystery, but they are not perfect. The three members of the Trinity **are not** three different parts of God. Each Person is equal. They are each 100% completely God and complete on their own. God doesn't change. He exists as ONE God and THREE persons all at once!

We will learn more about this next week.

WRITE what you learned.

LEARN: Write Acts 16:31 below from memory, if you can.

"_ _ _ _ _ _ _   _ _   _ _ _   _ _ _ _

_ _ _ _ _   _ _ _ _ _,   _ _ _   _ _ _

_ _ _ _   _ _   _ _ _ _ _."

A _ _ _   _ _: _ _.

PRAY: Pray for your family. Write your prayer requests, look back at your past requests, and write any answers below.

PRAYER REQUESTS:

ANSWERS to PRAYERS:

SATURDAY.

Today is a catch-up day if you missed a day.

If you are all caught up, here is a fun activity for you to do.

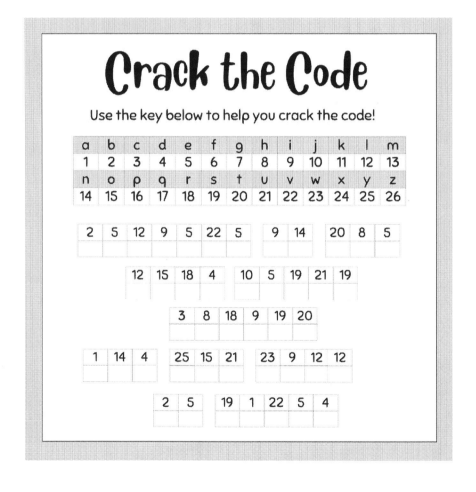

Crack the Code

Use the key below to help you crack the code!

a	b	c	d	e	f	g	h	i	j	k	l	m
1	2	3	4	5	6	7	8	9	10	11	12	13
n	o	p	q	r	s	t	u	v	w	x	y	z
14	15	16	17	18	19	20	21	22	23	24	25	26

2 5 12 9 5 22 5   9 14   20 8 5

12 15 18 4   10 5 19 21 19

3 8 18 9 19 20

1 14 4   25 15 21   23 9 12 12

2 5   19 1 22 5 4

SUNDAY

Today is Sunday. Spend time talking about what you learned in church and/or Sunday School.

WEEK THREE

God the Father.

God the Son.

God the Holy Spirit.

Does God Like Me?

MONDAY

FUN QUESTION: Which of your friends is easiest to talk to? Why?

READ: 1 John 3:1-3.

READ the devotion below.

GOD - THE FATHER

God is the Father of all and the BEST FRIEND you could ever have. He is just one Member of the Trinity.

The whole Trinity idea is confusing, isn't it?
Will we be able to understand better when we get older? No, because our brains cannot fully understand an infinite, invisible, immeasurable God.

"How great God is! We'll never completely understand Him."
Job 36:26 (NIRV).

God is our Father, the Creator of the earth, the almighty King of Kings.

He is Jesus, who came to earth as a baby and died for our sins.

He is the Holy Spirit who is always with us to provide comfort and help.

It's impossible for us to wrap our human minds around the God of the world. But we can trust Him!

The Bible tells us that God is a good and perfect FATHER. What are some qualities of a good father?

____

____

____

Some kids don't have great dads, and many live with just their moms, which can be really hard.

But God can fill any emptiness that a father's absence may leave behind.

READ Isaiah 64:7 and Psalm 68:5

God is a F __ __ __ __ __ to the fatherless.

He is the best Father ever - for everyone!

WRITE what you learned.

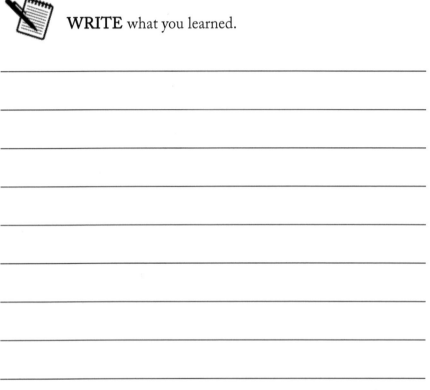

LEARN: Begin learning Proverbs 3:5-6.

PRAY: Pray for your friends.

Write your prayer requests, look back at your past requests, and write any answers below.

PRAYER REQUESTS:

ANSWERS to PRAYERS:

TUESDAY

FUN QUESTION: What activities would you plan if you could have a special day dedicated to you?

READ: John 1:14.

READ the devotion below.

GOD - THE SON - JESUS

Did you know that Jesus became a man and walked on earth, just like we do?

He was born ("became flesh"), lived like us, and then He died. He did normal things each day, like eating, playing, and sleeping. He was a person, and yet He is also God.

He is called the "Son of God." He is also called "The Word." His name is JESUS.

READ 1 John 5:20.

He is the T __ __ __ G __ __.

READ Hebrews 4:15-16.

Because He lived a life just like us, Jesus understands the temptations and struggles that we face.

WRITE what you learned.

LEARN: Keep learning Proverbs 3:5-6.

PRAY: Pray for your Grandparents.

Write your prayer requests, look back at your past requests, and write any answers below.

PRAYER REQUESTS:

ANSWERS to PRAYERS:

WEDNESDAY

FUN QUESTION: Do you get more excited on your birthday or your best friend's birthday? Why?

READ: 1 Corinthians 2:10-12.

READ the devotion below.

GOD THE HOLY SPIRIT.

Jesus had birthrequests, just like we do, because He became a man. He is a God-Man.

Yet God was more than that.
He is also the Holy Spirit.

You might not have heard about the Holy Spirit, so let's learn a bit about Him.

What are some of the things that the Holy Spirit does?

READ these verses.

John 14:26.

The Holy Spirit is our H __ __ __ __ __ and T __ __ __ __ __ __ __ __.

John 16:13.

The Holy Spirit will G __ __ __ __ us in to T __ __ __ __.

Ephesians 4:30.

The Holy Spirit P __ __ __ __ for us.

We may not be able to see the Holy Spirit, but He is always there.

WRITE what you learned.

LEARN: Keep learning Proverbs 3:5-6.

PRAY: Pray for your school teachers.

Write your prayer requests, look back at your past requests, and write any answers below.

PRAYER REQUESTS:

ANSWERS to PRAYERS:

THURSDAY

FUN QUESTION: If you were a parent, what new rules would you make for your family? Which ones would you ditch?

READ: What new rules would you make for your family if you were a parent? Which ones would you ditch?

READ the devotion below.

THE TRINITY - THREE IN ONE

Sometimes, our parents' rules don't seem to make sense to us. They are older and wiser, and it might take a while for us to understand fully.

Understanding God is even more difficult.
God the Father, God the Son, and God the Spirit are not three Gods but the same God.

Will we be able to understand this better when we get older? Not really, because our brains cannot fully understand an infinite, invisible, immeasurable God.
We can get to know God, but we will never be able to fully understand Him.

He is the Creator of the world, the almighty King of Kings. It's impossible for us to wrap our human minds around the God of the universe.

But we can trust Him!

WRITE what you learned.

LEARN: Keep learning Proverbs 3:5-6.

SCAN ME

PRAY: Pray for your church.

Write your prayer requests, look back at your past requests, and write any answers below.

PRAYER REQUESTS:

ANSWERS to PRAYERS:

FRIDAY

FUN QUESTION: If you could only eat one food for the rest of your life, what would it be?

READ: 1 John 3:1.

READ the devotion below.

DOES GOD LOVE ME?

Thank goodness we don't have to eat the same food every day, forever.

God loved us enough to create a HUGE variety.

So, the most important question of them all is, "Does God love me?"

YES! YES! YES!!

GOD LOVES YOU! It's the best news of all!

- The God of the universe loves you.
- The Creator of the whole world loves you!
- The King of Kings loves YOU.

The word "lavished" in our verse today means, "heaped," poured," or "smothered."

What does this mean?

Which do you like more?

- ☐ Mashed potatoes smothered with gravy?
- ☐ Or ice cream smothered with chocolate sauce?

God has "smothered" you with His love. That's a LOT of love!

WRITE what you learned.

LEARN: Keep learning Proverbs 3:5-6.

SCAN ME

PRAY: Pray for your Sunday School teacher. Write your prayer requests, look back at your past requests, and write any answers below.

PRAYER REQUESTS:

____

____

____

____

ANSWERS to PRAYERS:

____

____

____

____

SATURDAY.

Today is a catch-up day if you missed a day.

If you are all caught up, here is a fun activity for you to do.

Word Scramble

Unscramble the following words about God.

1. RELEPH
2. HRETACR
3. SJUSE
4. EGUDIS
5. INEDFR
6. YNTIRTI
7. NOS
8. RTEHFA
9. YOHL PRSITI
10. YPARS

SUNDAY

Today is Sunday. Spend time talking about what you learned in church and/or Sunday School.

WEEK FOUR

Does God Love Me?

Bad News & Good News.

MONDAY

FUN QUESTION: Who do you love the most? Why?

READ: Zephaniah 3:17

READ the devotion below.

DOES GOD LIKE ME?

God doesn't just love you. He LIKES you, too! In fact, He DELIGHTS in you!

God likes you more than you can imagine.
He should because He created you!
He made you exactly how He wanted you to be.
And God DOESN'T make mistakes!

READ Psalm 139:13-14.
You have been fearfully and W __ __ __ __ __ __ __ __ __ __ made!

READ Matthew 10:30.

God also knows everything about you, even how many H __ __ __ __ are on your head!

God is the PERFECT Father.

WRITE what you learned.

LEARN: Fill in the words to your memory verse.

SCAN ME

"T __ __ __ __ in the Lord with A __ __ your heart and lean not on your own understanding; in A __ __ your ways S __ __ __ __ __ to Him, and He will make your paths straight."

Proverbs 3:5-6.

PRAY: Pray for your enemies.

Write your prayer requests, look back at your past requests, and write any answers below.

PRAYER REQUESTS:

ANSWERS to PRAYERS:

TUESDAY

FUN QUESTION: What's the hardest thing you've learned to do?

READ: Isaiah 55:8-9.

READ the devotion below.

WHY DOES GOD LET BAD THINGS HAPPEN?

Sometimes, understanding is the hardest thing. We don't understand.

If God is love, then…

- Why did I get sick?
- Why did my friend die?
- Why did my parents get divorced?
- How can a loving God allow all of the evil, pain, and suffering in the world?

These are hard questions.

We cannot understand God's mind. But here is what the Bible tells us.

God created a perfect world, but Adam and Eve disobeyed.
Their sin changed everything
It introduced sickness, pain and death into the world.

We are sinners, just like Adam and Eve, and we live in a world that has been affected by sin.

So, God doesn't "cause" bad things. It's because of SIN!

WRITE what you learned.

LEARN: Review Acts 16:31

Fill in the words to this week's memory verse.

"T _ _ _ _ in the Lord with A _ _ your heart and lean not on

your own understanding;

in A _ _ your ways S _ _ _ _ _ to Him,

and He will make your paths straight."

Proverbs 3:5-6.

PRAY: Ask God to help you learn more about Him. Write your prayer requests, look back at your past requests, and write any answers below.

PRAYER REQUESTS:

ANSWERS to PRAYERS:

WEDNESDAY

FUN QUESTION: What would you invent if you could make any invention in the world?

READ: Romans 6:23.

READ the devotion below.

BAD NEWS

Imagine if you could invent a machine that would take away all of the sins in the world.

It would be a much better world, don't you think? God wants us to trust Him. But we have a problem. We are sinners, and the penalty for sin is D __ __ __ __.

Sin is when we do, say, or think anything wrong – anything that displeases God. Sin brought the horrible consequences of physical death and suffering.

But there is more bad news. We are also spiritually dead. God is a holy and just Judge, and we are separated from Him because of our sin.

That's B __ __ news!

WRITE what you learned.

LEARN: Review Acts 16:31. Fill in the words to this week's memory verse.

SCAN ME

"T __ __ __ __ in the Lord with A __ __ your heart and lean not on your own understanding; in A __ __ your ways S __ __ __ __ __ to Him, and He will make your paths straight."

Proverbs 3:5-6.

PRAY: Pray for your family.

Write your prayer requests, look back at your past requests, and write any answers below.

PRAYER REQUESTS:

ANSWERS to PRAYERS:

THURSDAY

FUN QUESTION: What cheers you up when you're sad?

READ: John 3:16-17

READ the devotion below.

GOOD NEWS.

What would you change if you could? God changed our sin penalty. He loves us so much that He sent His only Son, Jesus, to die in our place. Jesus paid our sin penalty so that we wouldn't have to.
How amazing is that!! Now we can go to be with Jesus in heaven FOREVER!

What do we need to do to get eternal life? (Circle the right answers).

Go to church?	Be good?
Love people?	Believe in Jesus?

READ John 3:16 again to check your answers.

WRITE what you learned.

LEARN: Review Acts 16:31. Fill in the words to this week's memory verse.

"T __ __ __ __ in the Lord with A __ __ your heart and lean not on your own understanding; in A __ __ your ways S __ __ __ __ __ to Him, and He will make your paths straight."

Proverbs 3:5-6.

PRAY: Pray for your friends.

Write your prayer requests, look back at your past requests, and write any answers below.

PRAYER REQUESTS:

ANSWERS to PRAYERS:

FRIDAY

FUN QUESTION: If you became President of the United States, what would you change?

READ: Revelation 21:1-4.

READ the devotion below.

GOOD NEWS

One day, Jesus will return to bring us to heaven. He will make a new heaven and earth for believers to enjoy forever, free from sin and sadness.

What is heaven like? READ these verses:

READ Revelation 4:3 and 4:6.

There is a T _ _ _ _ _ and a S _ _.

READ Revelation 5:11.

It is full of A _ _ _ _ _.

READ Revelation 21:25.

There will be no N __ __ __ __.

READ Revelation 21:4.

There will be NO MORE D __ __ __ __.

And best of all, Jesus is there. That is GREAT NEWS!

WRITE what you learned.

LEARN: Write Proverbs 3:5-6 below from memory (if you can!).

SCAN ME

"T __ __ __ __ in the Lord with A __ __ your heart and lean not on your own understanding; in A __ __ your ways S __ __ __ __ __ to Him, and He will make your paths straight."

Proverbs 3:5-6.

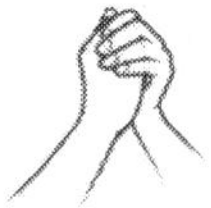

PRAY: Pray for your Grandparents. Write your prayer requests, look back at your past requests, and write any answers below.

PRAYER REQUESTS:

____

____

____

____

____

____

ANSWERS to PRAYERS:

____

____

____

____

____

SATURDAY.

Today is a catch-up day if you missed a day.

If you are all caught up, here is a fun activity for you to do.

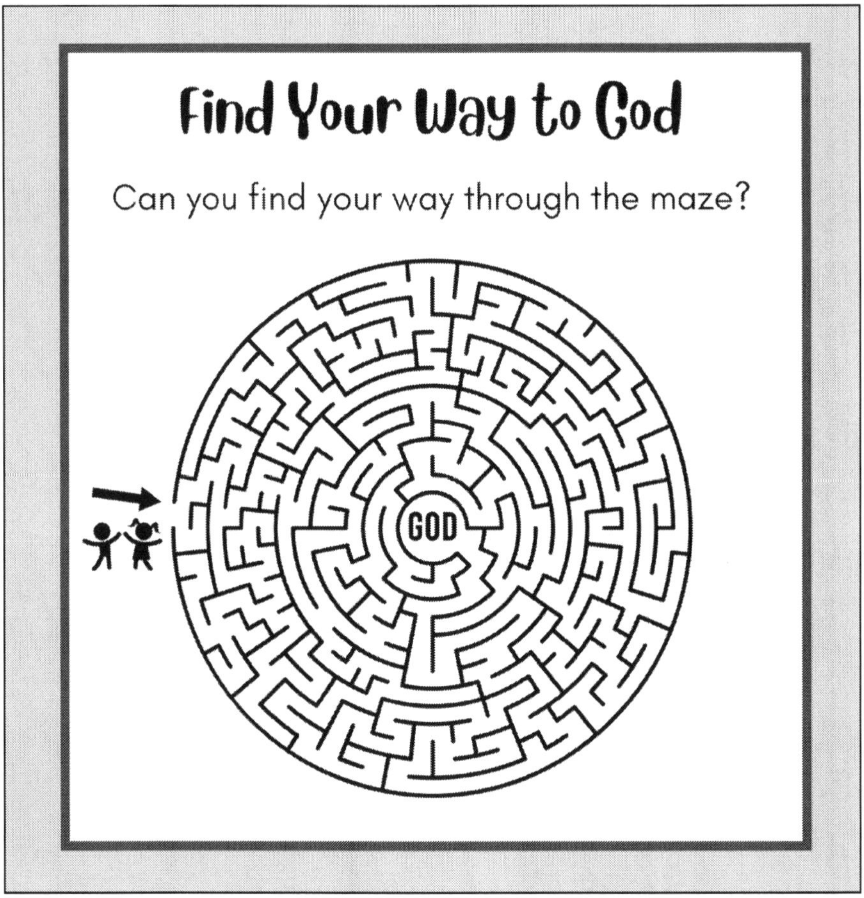
Find Your Way to God
Can you find your way through the maze?
GOD

SUNDAY

Today is Sunday.

Spend time talking about what you learned in church and/or Sunday School.

____

____

____

____

Review both of your memory verses.

Write Proverbs 3:5-6 below from memory.

“T _ _ _ _ in the Lord with A _ _ your heart and lean not on

your own understanding;

in A _ _ your ways S _ _ _ _ _ to Him,

and He will make your paths straight.”

Proverbs 3:5-6.

Write Acts 16:31 below from memory.

"_ _ _ _ _ _ _ _ _ _ _ _ _ _ _ _ _ _ _

_ _ _ _ _ _ _ _ _ _ _ _ _, _ _ _ _ _ _

_ _ _ _ _ _ _ _ _ _ _ _ _ _."

A _ _ _ _ _: _ _.

CONGRATULATIONS

You have completed "UNDERSTANDING GOD," the first "10 Minutes with God" book.

Don't stop now! Complete all seven.

1. Understanding God – Can I Trust Him?
2. Knowing God - Can I Know for Sure?
3. Following God – What Do I Do?
4. Understanding the Bible – How Do I Know it's True?

5. Understanding Me (Identity) – Who Am I?
6. Understanding Big Questions – I Need Answers.
7. Understanding Life & Death – What Happens When We Die?

ANSWER KEY

Week One.

Thursday. Leave.

Friday. All, Beginning, End.

Week Two.

Monday. Everything.

Wednesday. Princes, Rulers, Hands, Strong, Mighty, Battle, Love, Pray.

Thursday. None.

Friday. Three, Three, Three, Father, Son, Holy Spirit.

Week Three.

Monday. Father.

Tuesday. True God.

Wednesday. Helper, Teacher, Guide, Truth, Prayers.

Week Four.

Tuesday. Wonderfully.

Wednesday. Death, Bad.

Friday. Throne, Sea, Angels, Night, Death.

Week One Answers

G	R	G	W	C	A	T
O	P	H	I	E	R	F
D	S	T	N	N	O	A
E	I	R	D	T	M	I
P	R	E	S	E	N	T
U	A	A	O	E	I	H
V	I	S	I	B	L	E

Week Two Answers

2	5	12	9	5	22	5
B	e	l	i	e	v	e

9	14
i	n

20	8	5
t	h	e

12	15	18	4
L	o	r	d

10	5	19	21	19
J	e	s	u	s

3	8	18	9	19	20
C	h	r	i	s	t

1	14	4
a	n	d

25	15	21
y	o	u

23	9	12	12
w	i	l	l

2	5
b	e

19	1	22	5	4
s	a	v	e	d

Week 3 Answers

1. RELEPH	HELPER
2. HRETACR	TEACHER
3. SJUSE	JESUS
4. EGUDIS	GUIDES
5. INEDFR	FRIEND
6. YNTIRTI	TRINITY
7. NOS	SON
8. RTEHFA	FATHER
9. YOHL PRSITI	HOLY SPIRIT
10. YPARS	PRAYS

ABOUT THE AUTHOR

Originally a high school teacher in her native Australia, Janine McNally has partnered together with her husband for many years of pastoral ministry.

Janine graduated with a Master of Theology from Dallas Theological Seminary and a Doctor of Ministry from Grace School of Theology.

She is the author of "When You See Fireflies—Equipping Leaders and Parents to Minister Effectively to Generation Alpha" and the accompanying Leader's Guide, "An Empty Crib – A Survival Guide to Losing a Child," as well as seven books in the "Understanding Life for Kids" series and the "STEPS to Knowing Jesus" series for kids and preteens.

Her current project is to create Family Devotion Cards to help parents fulfill their biblical role of passing along their faith to their children and grandchildren.

"And these words which I command you today shall be in your heart. You shall teach them diligently to your children, and shall talk of them when you sit in your house, when you walk by the way, when you lie down, and when you rise up.
You shall bind them as a sign on your hand, and they shall be as frontlets between your eyes. You shall write them on the doorposts of your house and on your gates."
Deuteronomy 6:6-9

She passionately believes in reaching kids for Jesus and enlightening leaders and parents about Generation Alpha and beyond.

Janine and Gary have been married for thirty-one years and live in Panama City, Florida. They have three grown children, Hannah (married to Kevin), Jonathan, and Jami, and three beautiful grandchildren, Grayson, Hunter, and Emerson.

ABOUT THE ORGANIZATION

Janine McNally directs the operations of **Equipping Fireflies**, a non-profit dedicated to providing gospel-centered resources that proclaim a message that will grab the attention of this generation, break the magnetic attraction of the increasingly dark world, and lead children to the Light.

THE STORY BEHIND THE NAME

"When do we have to come inside?"
"When you see the fireflies."

Our kids loved to play outside, but as night began to fall, it was time to come in, where it was safe. Each evening, for a short time, the fireflies would light up our entire backyard. Their unmistakable glow was the signal that it was time.

Our world has become much darker. We desperately need the kids and their families to hear the call. "Come inside where it's safe." The world is rapidly becoming bleaker as the generations race by, yet our children are running towards the night.

We must proclaim a message that grabs their attention, one that they understand and that will break the magnetic attraction of the increasingly dark world.

"You are the light of the world.
Let your light shine before others that they may see your good deeds and glorify your Father in heaven."
Matthew 5:14; 16

OUR PASSION

Statistics show that most Christians trusted Christ between the ages of 3 and 12. Our passion is to reach children for Jesus and serve, equip, and encourage Children's Ministry leaders and parents.

THE GOOD NEWS

When Jesus died on the cross, He did EVERYTHING that God requires for us to go to heaven when we die."

Lighting the Way for the Next Generations.

https://www.equippingfireflies.com

ENDNOTES

---

[1] cf. Deuteronomy 11:18-21; 32:45-46.

[2] What would Jesus do?

[3] D. K. Steele, 'A Biblical and Theological Rationale for A Familial Motif of Congregational Life That Facilitates the Transfer of Faith from Generation to Generation.'

[4] "For I have known Him [God], in order that he [Dad] may command his children and his household after him [grandchildren], that they keep the way of the Lord." Genesis 18:19

"And that you [Parent] may tell in the hearing of your son and your son's son [grandson] the mighty things I [God] have done in Egypt..." Exodus 10:2.

"And teach them [God's commands] to your children and your grandchildren." Deuteronomy 4:9.

[5] C. M. Anderson, *Education Is Discipleship: So, Who's Really Discipling Your Kids?*

[6] The complete Bible verses have been omitted so you could teach your child how to use a physical Bible.

[7] Hebrews 11:1.

Made in the USA
Columbia, SC
07 March 2025

54746895R00076